CHICK HENN

The Easter Egg
Joke Book

Illustrations by Rowan Barnes-Murphy

FANTAIL

FANTAIL PUBLISHING,
AN IMPRINT OF PUFFIN ENTERPRISES

Published by the Penguin Group
27 Wrights Lane, London W8 5TZ England

Viking Penguin Inc., 40 West 23rd Street New York, NY10010, USA.
Penguin Books Australia Ltd. Ringwood, Victoria, Australia.
Penguin Books Canada Ltd., 2801 John Street, Markham, Ontario, Canada LR3 1BA.
Penguin Books (NZ) Ltd., 182-190 Wairau Road Auckland 10 New Zealand.
Penguin Books Ltd., Registered Offices: Harmondsworth, Middlesex, England.

First Published by Penguin Books Ltd, 1990

13579108642

Text copyright © Signpost Books Ltd, 1990
Illustrations copyright © Rowan Barnes-Murphy, 1990
Design; Gillian Riley
Cover Design; Dave Crook
Cover Illustration; Kim Blundell
All rights reserved.

0140 902864

Printed and bound in Great Britain by
William Clowes Limited, Beccles and London

Eggs Eleven

Humpty Dumpty sat on a wall
Humpty Dumpty had a great fall
All the king's horses, and all the king's men
Had scrambled eggs for breakfast again.

ANY SECOND NOW!

There were two eggs boiling in a saucepan.
'Phew, it's hot in here,' said one.
'Wait till you get out,' said the other.
'You'll get your head bashed in.'

Why are eggs like bricks?
They have to be laid.

What's a fighter pilot's favourite breakfast?
Scrambled eggs.

Do Daleks like eggs?
No. They eggsterminate them.

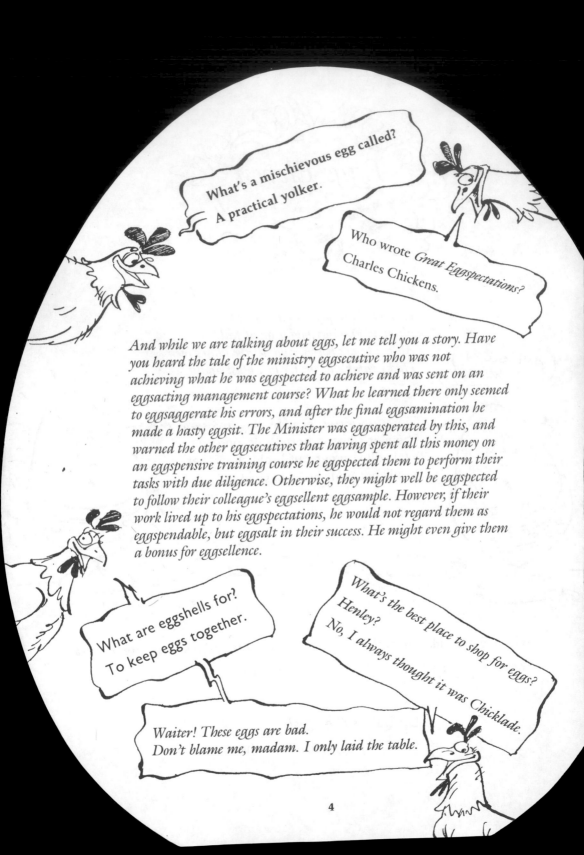

What's a mischievous egg called?
A practical yolker.

Who wrote *Great Eggspectations*?
Charles Chickens.

And while we are talking about eggs, let me tell you a story. Have you heard the tale of the ministry eggsecutive who was not achieving what he was eggspected to achieve and was sent on an eggsacting management course? What he learned there only seemed to eggsaggerate his errors, and after the final eggsamination he made a hasty eggsit. The Minister was eggsasperated by this, and warned the other eggsecutives that having spent all this money on an eggspensive training course he eggspected them to perform their tasks with due diligence. Otherwise, they might well be eggspected to follow their colleague's eggsellent eggsample. However, if their work lived up to his eggspectations, he would not regard them as eggspendable, but eggsalt in their success. He might even give them a bonus for eggsellence.

What are eggshells for?
To keep eggs together.

What's the best place to shop for eggs?
Henley?
No, I always thought it was Chicklade.

Waiter! These eggs are bad.
Don't blame me, madam. I only laid the table.

What is yellow and highly dangerous?
An eggs-ocet missile.

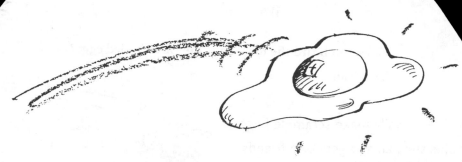

Do you say the yolk of an egg is white, or the yolk of an egg are white?
Neither.*

Mary: If I lay one egg on this chair and two on the table, how many will I have altogether?

Ann: Personally I don't believe you can do it.

The yolk of an egg is yellow.

A wee wee house
Fou, fou o' meat
Neither door nor window
To let you in to eat.

What is it? *

Have you heard the one about the three boiled eggs?
Two bad!

How does a wally make scrambled eggs?
He holds the pan and gets two friends
to shake him violently.

How do monsters like their eggs?
Terrifried.

EGGSCUSE ME!

What's yellow and highly dangerous?
A big eggsplosion.

If an egg came floating down the river Thames, where would it have come from?
A chicken.

What's the best way to make an egg roll?
Push it down the hill.

What's the smell of bad eggs?
Extinct (eggs-tinct).

Why is a wild pony like an egg?
Both must be broken before they can be used.

* an egg

Easter Eggstravaganza

What do you get if you pour hot water down a rabbit hole?

Hot cross bunnies.

Susan: The hens are putting on a show in the barn tonight.
Do you want to come?
Charlie: Will it be any good?
Susan: They say it will be a real Easter eggstravaganza!

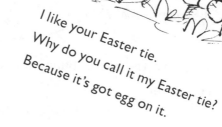

Why does everyone want to spend Easter with the mushroom?

Because he's a fungi to be with.

I like your Easter tie.
Why do you call it my Easter tie?
Because it's got egg on it.

Knock Knock.
Who's there?
Cook.
Cook who?
That's the first one I've heard this spring.

7

What happened when the chicken sat on the Easter Egg?
It melted.

How do you stop the cock crowing on Easter Monday morning?
Eat him for Sunday lunch.

Did you hear what happened at the milking contest
at the Easter show?
No.
Udder chaos.

Where do the lambs do their Easter shopping?
Wool-worths.

What did the rabbit do when his sister ate his Easter egg?
Thumper.

What is made of chocolate, has a peanut in the middle,
and sings hymns?
A Sunday School Treet.

HOW EGGCEEDINGLY RUDE!

What did the Easter bunny say to the lollipop?
Hi, sucker.

What is chocolate and lies on the ocean bed?
An Oyster egg.

Quick Quackers

What do you get if you cross a duck and a fire?

A fire quacker.

What do you get if you cross a whale and a duck?

Moby duckling.

What do you call a fast duck?

A quick quack.

Do ducks make wise quacks?

What bird grows up as it grows down?

A duckling.

Where do ducklings go when they are ill?

To the Ducktor.

A. QUACK

What's the best way to catch a wild duck?

Find a tame one and irritate it.

What language is quack quack?
Double duck.

Which duck takes a gun under his wing when he flies?
A high quacker.

What dance do ducks prefer?
The quack step.

What did the duck say when she bought some lipstick?
Put it on the bill.

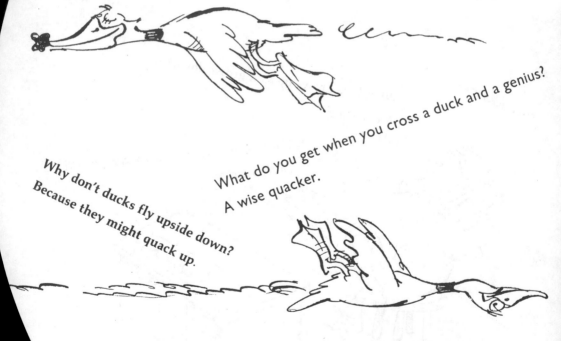

What do you get when you cross a duck and a genius?
A wise quacker.

Why don't ducks fly upside down?
Because they might quack up.

A duckling goes into the library each day, taking back one book and getting out another. The librarian is so curious she follows the duckling one day. The duckling goes up to a large frog sitting on a lily pad with a pile of books saying 'Read it, read it.'

Susan: Help! The cat's just eaten a duck.
Charlie: Does that make it a duck-filled fattypuss?

Do ducks make good decorators?
No, they just paper over the quacks.

What did the duckling say when she came out of the egg?
That was an eggsperience.

What's the difference between a goose and a duck?
A duck goes 'quack' and a goose goes 'honk.'
So what would you do if you were out for a walk and you
saw a flock of birds going 'honk, honk'?

I'd move and let them pass.

What are ducks' favourite television programmes?
Duckumentaries.

11

Crack a Yolk

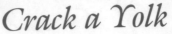

What goes cluck, cluck, bang?
A chicken in a minefield.

What's the definition of five chickens pecking at one worm?
Fowl play.

What did the chicken say to the miser?
Cheep, cheep.

What do chickens watch on television?
The Feather Forecast.

How did the chicken farmer wake up in the morning?
He had an alarm cluck.

One of Farmer Brown's chickens tried to run away yesterday.
She was fed up with being cooped up.

Fred: My chicken lays square eggs.
Alf: That's amazing! Can it talk too?
Fred: Yes, but just one word. 'Ouch.'

What happened to the newly hatched egg?
It chickened out.

Do chickens get people pox?

What do you get if you cross a chicken with a guitar?
A bird that makes music when you pluck it.

Why did the chicken cross the road?
For its own fowl reasons.

Why did the chicken cross the road?
To escape from Colonel Sanders.

Have you ever seen a man-eating tiger?
No, but I've seen a man eating chicken.

Cross a chicken with a turkey and what do you get?
A churkey.

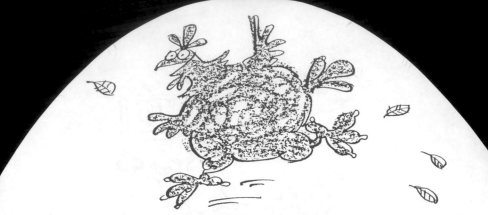

If the chicken crosses the road, rolls in the mud, and comes back, what do you get?
A dirty double-crosser.

What do you call a greasy chicken?
A slick chick.

When chicken broth was first tinned everybody thought it was souper!

What is the best time to buy chickens?
When they are going cheep.

I want to buy a chicken.
Do you want a pullet?
No, I'll take it home in my bag.

Why did the chicken go half-way across the road?
Because she wanted to lay it on the line.

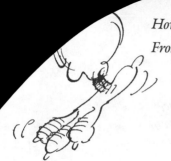

How do chickens start a race?

From scratch.

Cynthia: Isn't it wonderful how chickens get out of their shells?
Tony: It's even more wonderful how they get in.

Why did the lady blush when she passed the chicken coop?

She couldn't help overhearing the fowl language.

Chris: I see you've persuaded your neighbour to keep his chickens in the run, at last. How did you do it?
Linda: I hid a dozen eggs in the garden last night, and made sure he saw me collect them this morning.

What do you get if you cross a chicken with an octopus?

A chicken that means the whole family can have a leg at lunchtime.

I had a little chicky.
It wouldn't lay an egg.
Poured hot water
Up and down its leg.

Little chicky cried.
Little chicky begged.
Little chicky laid
A hard-boiled egg.

Mary had a little lamb
She ate it with mint sauce.
Everywhere that Mary went
The lamb went too, of course!

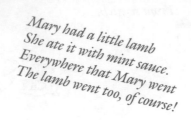

Mary had a little lamb
It leaped around in hops.
It gambolled in the road one day
And watch out . . . lamb chops.

Mary had a little lamb
Her father shot it dead.
And now it goes to school with her
Between two lumps of bread.

Mary had a Little Lamb ...

Mary had a little lamb
Which was an awful glutton.
It quickly grew into a sheep
And ended up as mutton.

Mary had a little lamb
You've heard this tale before
But did you know she passed her plate
And had a little more?

MORE PLEASE!

Some say that fleas are black
I know that is not so.
'Cos Mary had a little lamb
with fleas as white as snow.

Mary had a little lamb.
Charlie had a pup.
Michael had a crocodile
Which ate the others up.

Mary had a little lamb
It had a touch of colic.
She gave it brandy twice a day
Now its alcoholic.

Mary had a crocodile
That ate a child each day
But interfering people came
And took her pet away.

Fowl Play

Why did the chicken cross the road?
To get the Chinese newspaper.
Do you get it?
No.
Neither do I. We get *The Independent.*

What did the drunken chicken lay?

Scotch eggs.

Why did the chicken cross the road?
To practise her running.

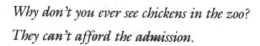

Why don't you ever see chickens in the zoo?
They can't afford the admission.

What do you call the ghost of a chicken?
A poultrygeist.

Why did the blind chicken cross the road?
To get to the bird's eye shop.

What did the chicken say when it found a lemon in the nest?
Look at the lemon mama laid.

What do you get if you cross a chicken with a banjo?
A chicken that plucks itself.

Why did the chicken run onto the football pitch?
The referee called a fowl.

Why did all the farmyard animals groan?
The chicken cracked a rotten yolk.

The chickens have decided they would like to play football.
Why?
Because there are ducks in cricket!

The chickens are holding a trial, as one of them has committed a murder.
What will happen?
The guilty one will be eggsecuted.

First chicken: I've just laid an egg 10cms long!
No one can beat that.
Second chicken: Mrs. Thompson can.
First chicken: How?
Second chicken: With an egg-beater.

Joan: I made a chicken pie but the dog got it.
Sam: Don't worry. We can always get another dog.

Where do cockerels go when they lose their knees?

To London. There are lots of cock-neys there!

Susan: That chicken's a tough character.
Charlie: Yes, he came from a hard-boiled egg.

Susan: I made a terrible mistake last week. I fed
the chickens with sawdust.
Charlie: What happened?
Susan: The eggs hatched this morning and we've got
nine chicks and a woodpecker.

That chicken is a champion boxer.
No.
Yes – the featherweight champion of the world!

Why did the beatnik chicken cross the road?

Because it was a lay-about.

What did the cobbler say when a flock of chickens
came into his workshop?

Shoo!

'Ears Laughing at you, Mate!

How do rabbits travel?
By hare plane.

Is running a rabbit farm a hare-raising experience?

How do rabbits keep their fur tidy?
With a hare brush.

The rabbit has a shiny nose
A fault he cannot mend
Because his little powder puff
Is at the other end.

What did the bunny want to be when he grew up?
He wanted to join the hare force.

What do you get if you cross a bunny with leeks?
Bunions.

Did you hear about the two rabbits that got married
and went to Majorca for their bunnymoon?

What do you call a rabbit with fleas?
Bugs Bunny.

How do rabbits and hares make beer?
They start with hops.

What happens to a rabbit when it gets very cross?
It gets hoppin' mad.

I'M SO MAD!

A man walked into the doctor's surgery with a baby rabbit growing out of his head.
'That's incredible,' said the doctor.
'Yes,' replied the rabbit. 'It was only a pimple on my bottom last night.'

Is it true that carrots are good for the eyesight?
Well, you never see a rabbit wearing glasses.

What do you call a bald rabbit?
Hareless.

25

What do you call a rabbit who inspects holes?
A burrow surveyor.

What do you call a super-rich rabbit?
A millionhare.

Why did the rabbit cross the road?
To show he had guts.

What is a twip?
A twip is what a wabbit takes when he wides a twain.

Who looks after the money in a rabbit warren?
The burrow treasurer.

How do you catch a rabbit?
Hide in the grass and make a noise like lettuce.

What did one floppy-eared bunny say to another floppy-eared bunny?
'Ears looking at you, mate.

Waiter, waiter, there's no rabbit in this rabbit pie!
Well, you don't get any dog in dog biscuits, do you?

What does the baby rabbit do when it rains?

Gets wet.

Teacher: **If I give you three baby rabbits, and then tomorrow another five baby rabbits, how many will you have?**
Angus: **Thirteen.**
Teacher: **Thirteen?**
Angus: **Yes. I've got five already.**

What's the difference between a crazy rabbit and a forged five-pound note?

One's a mad bunny and the other is bad money.

Waiter, waiter, what's this thing singing hymns on my plate?

A welsh rabbit, sir.

What's the name of a chap with a rabbit sitting on his head?

Warren.

Which are the world's most mathematical animals?
Rabbits – because they keep on multiplying.

How do you say 'rabbit' without using the letter 'R'?
Bunny.

Mother rabbit was having trouble with her children, who
kept on asking where they had come from.
'I'm far too busy to answer that question at the moment,'
said Mother rabbit.
'Please, Mum,' said the little rabbits. 'Please tell us.'
'All right,' said the mother rabbit. 'If you must know,
you were all pulled out of a magician's hat!'

Why did the bald man put a rabbit on his head?
Because he thought it would give him a head of hare.

The hares have escaped!
Quick! Comb the area.

Don't Knock the Knock!

Knock, knock.
Who's there?
Alcott.
Alcott who?
Alcott the cake. You pour the tea.

Knock, knock.
Who's there?
Mike Howe.
Mike Howe who?
Mike Howe is sick.

Knock, knock.
Who's there?
Buck.
Buck who?
'Buck, buck!' I'm a chicken.

Knock, knock.
Who's there?
Adelaide.
Adelaide who?
Adelaide an egg.

Knock, knock.
Who's there?
Eggs.
Eggs who?
Eggs-tremely cold out here in the chicken house.

Knock, knock.
Who's there?
Andy Green.
Andy Green who?
"Andy green grass grows all around, all around . . ."

Knock, knock.
Who's there?
Barbie.
Barbie who?
Barbie Q. Chicken.

Knock, knock.
Who's there?
Easter.
Easter who?
Easter anybody home?

THATS EGGSCRUCIATING!

Knock, knock.
Who's there?
Henny.
Henny who?
Henny Penny. The sky is falling down!

Knock, knock.
Who's there?
Izzy.
Izzy who?
Izzy end of the world!

Knock, knock.
Who's there?
Yvette.
Yvette who?
Yvette fixed her up.

Knock, knock.
Who's there?
Ollie or Rex.
Ollie or Rex who?
Don't put Ollie or Rex in one basket.

Knock, knock.
Who's there?
Vilma.
Vilma who?
Vilma frog turn into a prince?

Knock, knock.
Who's there?
Egbert.
Egbert who?
Egbert no bacon.

That's eggsquisite!

Knock, knock.
Who's there?
Chesterfield.
Chesterfield who?
Chesterfield full of cows, that's all.

Funny Croaks

Where do tadpoles change into frogs?
In the croakroom.

What's a frog's favourite sweet?
A lollihop.

Where do frogs hang their coats?
In the croakroom (it's a busy place!).

What do frogs think in water?
They ponder.

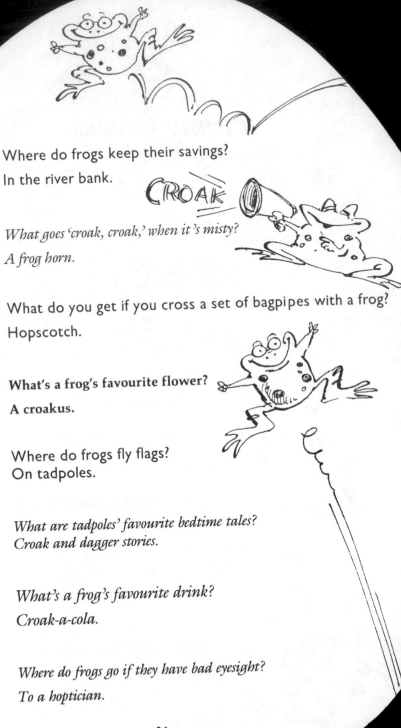

Where do frogs keep their savings?
In the river bank.

What goes 'croak, croak,' when it's misty?
A frog horn.

What do you get if you cross a set of bagpipes with a frog?
Hopscotch.

What's a frog's favourite flower?
A croakus.

Where do frogs fly flags?
On tadpoles.

What are tadpoles' favourite bedtime tales?
Croak and dagger stories.

What's a frog's favourite drink?
Croak-a-cola.

Where do frogs go if they have bad eyesight?
To a hoptician.

Easter Bon-Bons

What cake wanted to rule the world?
Attila the bun.

What do you get if you cross cocoa with an elk?
Chocolate mousse.

Why did the chocolate factory hire the farmer's daughter?
They needed someone to milk chocolates.

Which side of a round cake is the left side?
The side which isn't eaten.

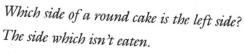

Why is a sponge cake like the sun?
Because it is light when it rises.

Who hold up trains but are never arrested?
Bridesmaids.

What do you do if somebody offers you a rock cake?
Take your pick.

What is the definition of a doughnut?
A crazy millionaire.

EEEEEK!

What did the big flower say to the little flower?
Hiya, bud.

What are the best things to put in a currant cake?
Your teeth.

Other Yolly Yolks

Why do chickens go to the theatre?
For their hentertainment.

What do you get if you cross a hen with a waiter?
Neatly laid eggs.

Cross a chef with a rooster and what do you get?
A cook-a-doodle-doo.

What did the Spanish farmer say to his hen?
Olé.

Who cracks yolks about chickens?
A comedihen.

Why did the hen sit on the axe?
So she could hatchet.

What happens when you cross a pooch with a hen?
You get pooched eggs.

What do you get when you cross a hen with a cement mixer?
A brick layer.

Why wouldn't the cockerel fight?
Because he was a chicken.

How do hens dance?
Chick to chick.

Why is it a waste of time having a party for hens?
Because it is difficult to make hens meet.

Have you heard about the lazy cockerel?
At daybreak he waits for the other cockerels to crow, and nods his head.

Why did the hens complain?
They were fed up with working for chicken feed.

What's the opposite of cock-a-doodle-doo?
Cock-a-doodle-don't.

Jim: What is that hen doing on your head?
Sally: I heard egg shampoo was good for your hair.

What do you call an intrepid hen?
An eggsplorer.

Why has that chicken got a red face?
It's henbarrassed.

Where do chickens live in New York?
The Henpire State Building.

What do you get if you cross a hen with an electric organ?
Hammond eggs.

City lady: How can I find out more about hens?
Farmer: You could try looking it up in the Hencyclopaedia.

What's the definition of impeccable?
Something hens can't eat.

The motorist ran over the farmer's hen, but offered to pay for it.
'I'll give you a pound,' he said to the farmer.
'You'll have to make it two pounds,' said the farmer.
'After all, you've killed two of my best birds.'
'What do you mean?' cried the motorist.
'Well, when the cockerel finds out, he'll die of sheer grief!'

A man bought ninety hens. He placed thirty on the first perch, thirty on the second perch, and the remaining thirty on the top perch.
Which hens did he own?
Only the ones on the first perch, because the others were on higher perches (hire purchase).

Why did the Navy cross hens with dynamite?
They wanted to get mine layers.

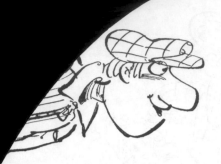

City dweller: Why do hens have such short legs?

Farmer: Because if they were taller, the eggs would smash with the fall.

Who conquered the world laying eggs all the way?

Attila the Hen.

Why do hens always lay in the daytime?

Because at night they become roosters.

Pickles: I'm worried about my brother. He's been thinking for years that he's a hen.
Doctor: Good gracious. Why didn't you come to me before about this?
Pickles: Well, we needed the eggs.

What's the poultry farmer's favourite drink?
A cocktail.

'What a good yolk,' he cracked.

Ewe've got to be Joking!

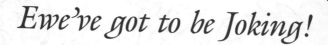

Why did Bo Peep lose her sheep?
She had a crook with her.

Cross a sheep with a kangaroo, and what do you get?

*A jumper with a pocket — and you thought I was going to say
a woolly jumper, didn't you?*

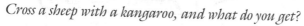

What's white and goes 'Baa, baa, splat!'
A sheep falling off a cliff.

How do sheep keep warm in winter?
Central bleating.

What do sheep look for at sales?
Baagains.

Do you know that it takes three sheep to make a jumper?
I didn't even know sheep could knit.

What do you get if you cross a sheep with a rainstorm?
A wet woolly blanket.

What do you get if you cross a sheep with an octopus?
A sweater with eight arms.

What do sheep say as they go through a gate?
After ewe.

Susan: That sheep behaves just like a person.
Charlie: Yes, she wants to be a eweman being.

Did you hear the story of the man who was trampled on when the flock of sheep stampeded?
No. What happened?
He was dyed in the wool.

Why are sheep like pubs?
They're full of baas.

What do lady shepherds wear?
Eweniforms.

What's the difference between a dog and a sheep?
One carries fleas and the other fleece.

Which shop do sheep like to go to?
The baabers.

A sheep farmer went to a vet and said he was having trouble with a ram who kept banging his head against a barn. The vet said that the ram probably had bad nerves, and that playing some music might help to soothe him.

Several weeks later the vet visited the farmer and found that the ram had died. 'Did you play him some music?' said the vet. 'Certainly,' said the farmer. 'What did you play?' 'I played a record of Ella Fitzgerald singing "There Will Never Be Another You".'

Pull the Udder One
or
You'll Never Bulleve it

There once was a man who said, 'How
Shall I manage to carry my cow?
For if I should ask it
To get in my basket,
'Twould make such a terrible row.'

What do you get if you cross a cow with a tortoise?

Long-life milk.

The new farmhand asked the farmer how long cows should be milked.
The farmer replied, 'The same as short ones, of course.'

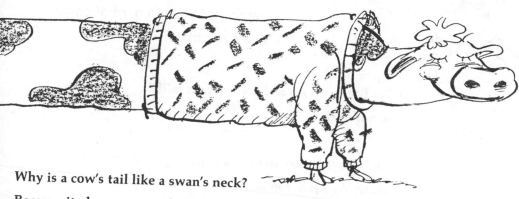

Why is a cow's tail like a swan's neck?

Because it always grows down.

Girl: I say, what a lovely coloured cow over there.
Boy: It's a Jersey.
Girl: Really? I thought it was its skin!

Why did the cow jump over the Moon?
Because there was no other way round.

51

Is a bull taking an afternoon nap a bulldozer?

Susan: This is funny tasting milk.
Charlie: Well, the cow's lost her memory.
Susan: Oh, you mean it's milk of amnesia.

What did the bull say to the cow?
When I fall in love it will be for heifer.

How do you count a herd of cows?
Use a cowculator of course.

What has one horn and gives lots of milk?
The milk van.

City lady: Is it easy to milk a cow?
Farmer: Any jerk can do it!

Which two animals always go with John wherever he goes?
His calves.

What do cows like doing on Saturday nights?
Going to the moovies.

Arthur: **Somebody's been stealing our cattle.**
Terry: **It must be the beefburglars.**

City lady: Those cows do seem to get on well together.
Farmer: Yes, ma'am. It's what you call cowperation.

What games do calves play at parties?
Moosical chairs.

Why did the cow sit on the spin dryer?
She wanted to make a milk shake.

What's a baby cow called?
Condensed milk.

Why do cows lie down in the rain?
To keep each udder warm.

Why did the cow slip away?
Because it saw the bull rush in.

What is a calf after it is one year old?
Two years old.

What happens if you walk under a cow?
You get a pat on the head.

Arthur: I gave that cow a five pound note to eat.
Terry: Why?
Arthur: To see if it made her milk richer.

4 stiff standers
4 lily-landers
2 lookers
2 crookers
And a wig-wag.

What am I?

A cow.

54

City lady: Look at that lovely bunch of cows.
Farmer: Not bunch – herd.
City lady: Herd of what?
Farmer: Herd of cows.
City lady: Of course I've heard of cows.
Farmer: No. A cow herd.
City lady: So what if it did? I've no secrets from a cow.

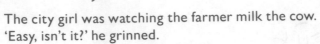

The city girl was watching the farmer milk the cow.
'Easy, isn't it?' he grinned.
'Seems to be,' said the girl. 'But how do you turn it off?'

What do you get if you cross a cow, a sheep and a goat?

The Milky Bar Kid.

Lambs' Tails

Customer: Do you serve lamb?
Waiter: I'm sorry, we don't allow animals to dine here.

Dopey Dan had two lambs, but he couldn't tell them apart. He finally decided to measure them, and that way he found out that the black lamb was 5cm taller than the white lamb.

Why was the lamb arrested by the motorway police?
For making a ewe turn.

Two lambs were gambolling on a hillside.
'Baa,' said the first lamb.
The second lamb said, 'Moo.'
The first lamb said, 'Baa.'
The second lamb replied, 'Moo.'
'Sheep don't say "moo",' the first lamb said.
'I know,' said the second lamb. 'I'm practising a foreign language.'

Why have farmers stopped wrapping their lambs in tissue paper when they send them to market?

To stop sheep rustling.

Where do lambs go on holiday?

The Baahaamaas.

Art Teacher: Why is your canvas blank? You were supposed to have painted a picture!
Student: This is a picture of a lamb grazing.
Art Teacher: Indeed – where is the grass?
Student: The lamb has eaten it.
Art Teacher: But where is the lamb?
Student: Well, you don't think she would stay there after eating all the grass, do you?

Pork Scratchings

Why wouldn't the piglets listen to their father?
He was an awful old boar.

What happened to the piglet who wanted to act in one of Shakespeare's plays?

He ended up as Hamlet and hogged the stage.

Why is a piglet like a bottle of ink?

Because it keeps going into the pen and then rushing out.

*Grandpa Grig had a pig
In a field of clover;
Piggie died, Grandpa cried,
And all the fun was over.*

If a farmer stands in his field with forty piglets,
how many feet have they got between them?

Two. Only the farmer has feet.

What's pink, has four legs and plays football?

Queen's Pork Rangers.

Arthur: We're running out of room to build new pig pens.
Terry: Perhaps we could build them one on top of the other.
Arthur: It could be the first styscraper!

What do you call the pigs' laundry?

Hogwash.

What's the definition of streaky bacon?

A pig running around with no clothes on.

Spring is Sprung

What is green and goes 'boing boing'?
Spring cabbage.

What did the baby's parents say?
After the Bawl is Over.

Der spring is sprung
Der grass is riz
I wonder where dem boidies is?

Der little boids is on der wing,
Ain't dat absoid?
Der little wings is on der boid!

Where are happy marriages made?
Gretna Grin.

How do you make a gardener angry?
Plant a foot in his seed bed.

Riddle me, riddle me
Riddle me ree.
I saw a nutcracker
Up a tree

What was it?*

What did the father goat say to the baby goat?
'You can't kid me.'

Is a baby budgerigar called a budget?

What did the nanny goat say to her badly behaved baby goat?
You're a crazy mixed-up kid.

Why was the young Scottish owl angry?
Because his mother wouldn't let him hoot at night.

* a squirrel

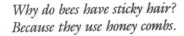

Why do bees have sticky hair?
Because they use honey combs.

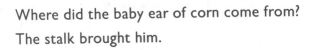

Where did the baby ear of corn come from?

The stalk brought him.

What did the baby hedgehog say when he backed into the cactus?

'Is that you, Mum?'

What do you get if you cross a piece of toast, an egg and a duvet?

Breakfast in bed.

The codfish lays 10,000 eggs
The lowly hen just one.
The codfish never cackles
To tell you what she's done.
And so we scorn the codfish
While the humble hen we prize.
Which only goes to show
That it pays to advertise.